Science Matters

Science and Design Technology in the Early Years

Linda Thornton and Pat Brunton

Science Matters

Science and Design Technology in the Early Years

Linda Thornton and Pat Brunton

TEACH BOOKS

A division of MA Education Ltd

Teach Books Division, MA Education Ltd, St Jude's Church,
Dulwich Road, London SE24 0PB

British Library Cataloguing-in-Publication Data
A catalogue record is available for this book

© Linda Thornton and Pat Brunton 2007

ISBN-10 1-85642-344-1
ISBN-13 978-1-85642-344-1

Printed in the UK by CLE, St Ives, Huntingdon, Cambridgeshire

Contents

Introduction

Young children as researchers and inventors

This book looks at ways to support young children as researchers and inventors as they develop their knowledge and understanding of the world in the foundation stage. Although the main emphasis is on science and design technology, there are also many examples of how to support a sense of time and place, personal social and emotional development and communication, language and literacy, as well as mathematical, creative and physical development.

Throughout the book we highlight the importance of adults and children learning together – co-constructing knowledge – and making use of opportunities for sustained shared thinking. Viewing children as researchers and inventors implies an awareness that children have their own ideas about how things work and why things happen – they are bubbling with ideas. Valuing these ideas and encouraging children to share them, as well as listening to the ideas put forward by others, provides a wealth of starting points for interesting investigations and discoveries.

The importance of the management of time, the organisation of the environment and the quality of the resources available for the children to use are exemplified in the practical ideas included in each chapter.

The structure of the book

Each chapter develops a particular theme and looks at the attitudes, skills and understanding which we as adults need in order to support young children as active, independent learners – young scientists and inventors. Alongside this is a selection of ideas and activities for you to use as starting points for encouraging children as researchers, exploring and investigating the world around them. At the end of each chapter there is a summary of key points which could provide useful starting points for discussion with colleagues.

Chapter 1 considers the vital role the adult plays in supporting the development of children's scientific and technological learning.

Chapter 2 discusses ways of fostering young children's curiosity and creating an environment for curiosity.

Chapter 3 looks at creativity and how important it is in scientific and technological learning.

Chapter 4 demonstrates the contribution made by the processes of science and technology in developing young children's communication skills.

Chapter 5 focuses on documentation and how it can be used to make children's scientific and technological learning visible.

Chapter 6 looks at the many different ways in which high quality display supports and celebrates children's learning.

Chapter 7 shows how careful planning of everyday experiences in a foundation stage setting can develop scientific and technological understanding, skills and dispositions.

Chapter 8 looks at 'finding the extraordinary in the ordinary, using collections of everyday objects as starting points for exploration and investigation.

Chapter 9 considers the importance of the outdoors, both natural spaces and the built environment.

Chapter 10 reviews the vital role that parents play in supporting their children's learning, and suggests interesting investigations to try at home.

Finally, *Chapter 11* summarises the contribution which exploration and investigation - science and design technology - make to young children's development as active and responsible citizens.

Chapter 1

The role of the adult

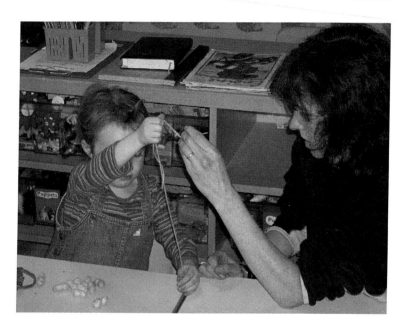

Young children come to science and technology with their own ideas and experience. Their knowledge will be as varied as that of the practitioners who work with them. As adults, we may have a deep interest and understanding of science and technology, or we may be uncertain, insecure or simply not interested in scientific and technological matters. However, one thing is certain: the attitude we adopt and the enthusiasm we display will provide the example that children will follow.

As adults, we often see children as having limited experience of science and technology. We think that they will benefit from learning what we know. Instead, we need to learn to view young children as competent learners, to trust their ideas and value their theories. By working this way, being confident to explore and learn alongside the children, we can enjoy the privilege of being partners in the knowledge building process.

Guided participation

As young children's skills and abilities develop they will enjoy working independently, but will still appreciate a little adult help on occasion. This is often a difficult situation to manage. Sensitivity is required to an individual child's need for support, knowing how to intervene without inhibiting thoughts and actions.

As a practitioner, you play a crucial role in supporting

the development of children's thinking and learning, by scaffolding their learning. Scaffolding is an interactive process where an adult and the child work alongside one another, with the adult's role being one of guided participation. To play this role successfully, you need to have a detailed understanding of where the child is, which will come from your close observation of individuals and groups of children.

In a setting which encourages investigation and exploration you, as an adult, will be aware of the importance of acting as a role model in all you do. By being curious yourself, by thinking out loud, by saying 'I wonder why...?' or 'What would happen if ...?' you are conveying important messages which the children will be aware of and begin to copy.

Remember that by not having all the answers, but instead by being an enthusiastic investigator alongside the children, you are playing a vital role in building their confidence as independent, self-confident learners.

From time to time there will be occasions when the children need to borrow your skills, knowledge and expertise. This brings us full circle to the importance of recognising when and how to share our skills, knowledge and understanding with children in a way that supports, but does not inhibit, their personal discoveries.

The role you choose to play

Working effectively with children involves adopting many different roles during the course of day. At different times you may be the motivator, communicator, expert, organiser or planner. Whichever role you are playing,

the way you choose to play it will be the key to creating a climate of enquiry where children can discover the wonders of the world around them.

Motivator

If you show interest in, and enthusiasm for, all that is happening in your setting, indoors and out, at different times of the day or the year, you will encourage the children to be involved, curious and questioning. For example, playing with shadows, experiencing the weather, noticing new buds and leaves or discovering how far a paper aeroplane will fly, are all exciting starting points for investigations. Remember, curiosity is contagious.

Therefore, as a motivator you will:

- Look for interesting starting points for investigation.

- Draw the children's attention to unusual happenings, such as a rainbow.
- Be interested and enthusiastic.

Communicator

In your role as communicator you will be actively listening as well as speaking, and encouraging the children to do the same. Active listening involves paying close attention to what children say and encouraging them to express their ideas in more depth. Show that you are listening carefully by your facial expressions, your body language and the words you use. Make sure that you give individual children the time that they need before responding.

Scientific enquiry is dependent upon the ability to ask questions, which can lead to interesting investigations and discoveries. As a good communicator you will ask fewer, better questions yourself and search for better answers from the children (see Chapter 4).

Value and provide opportunities for children to ask questions and remember to respond positively to children's spontaneous questions.

As a communicator you will:

- Be attentive to what children are telling you through all their different expressive languages.
- Ask open-ended questions that prompt enquiry and invite investigation.
- Model a questioning mind by thinking out loud.
- Introduce scientific and technical language which the children can use.
- Value time spent on discussion.

Expert or competent adult

As adults, you have the benefit of skills, knowledge and experience, which you have built up over time. Knowing how and when to use this expertise is crucial in supporting young children's scientific and technological learning.

There are skills that children need to acquire in order to be scientists. These include enquiry skills, practical skills and thinking and reasoning skills, all of which you will need to model for the children to see and imitate. Young children of today live in an increasingly technological world, and as they grow up they will experience developments in science and technology that we cannot even begin to imagine. As practitioners, we have a duty to equip ourselves with the scientific knowledge we need to guide and scaffold children's learning.

Skilful practitioners will be sensitive in the way in which they intervene in children's discoveries, knowing when to make to suggestions and when to stand back. Try tape recording your interactions with the children to recognise, and reflect on, the part you play in supporting their independent learning.

The competent adult will:

- Acquire the knowledge and skills needed to foster children's scientific and technological learning.
- Develop strategies to share skills and knowledge appropriately.
- Strive to improve the quality of interaction with the children.

Organiser

Creating an environment that fosters curiosity and encourages exploration and investigation needs careful organisation and management. The environment needs to be stimulating and challenging, as well as providing opportunities for children to make choices and take risks with their ideas. You need to consider the resources and equipment you provide, how you store them and how you ensure they are accessible to the children.

The organiser needs to:

- Arrange the environment so children can make real choices.
- Select appropriate resources, tools and equipment.
- Have procedures and policies in place which enable children to experience 'risky freedom'.
- Use interactive displays to encourage participation and question raising.

Planner

Good planning underpins scientific and technological teaching and learning, and facilitates all the roles described above. You should consider the starting points for investigations and the resources you might need; you also need to think about a range of other factors.

Effective scientific exploration and investigation take time and you need to find ways of giving children opportunities for extended enquiry and sustained thinking. Equally important, is to allow time for children to return to their discoveries and inventions and to refine their ideas.

How you group the children must be planned for (by interest, competence, social aptitude or possibly gender) to ensure that children are motivated and challenged.

Remember to build in opportunities for making children's learning visible. Include in your planning the ways in which you intend to observe and record children's learning processes and their knowledge and skills (see Chapter 5). Future planning will then be based on your interpretations of what the children have learned.

The planner will:

- Have a sound understanding of the learning intentions contained within knowledge and understanding of the world.
- Select the specific resources best suited to the chosen learning intention.
- Plan teaching strategies that will accommodate the different learning styles children use.
- Be flexible to give children the time they need to explore and discover.
- Vary the ways in which they group children.
- Develop competence in observing, recording and interpreting children's learning.
- Allow for, and welcome, the unexpected.

An example of the different roles in action

Creating a wildlife friendly garden

This example demonstrates the different roles you might play in relation to investigating living things around your setting.

Motivator: Designating a corner of your garden as a wildlife area will create a mini-habitat for many native plants and animals. As the motivator you might suggest the idea in the first place, arouse the enthusiasm of children and colleagues, and display the persistence needed to see the project through to completion.

Communicator: This project will provide many opportunities to develop communication skills. Consult the children about how they would like to develop the wildlife friendly area. Listen to the children's ideas about which animals they would like to attract to the garden and spend time discussing their suggestions. Help them to refine their ideas and make joint decisions about what is possible by carefully framing the questions you ask and sensitively challenging their thinking.

Expert or competent adult: As the competent adult, you will be in a position to advise on the best location for the garden and the types of plants that will attract insects. There will be opportunities to demonstrate the skills of digging, planting, lifting and carrying.

Organiser: Children can be involved in establishing the wildlife-friendly garden by planning where the different plants will go and then planting out and watering the new plants until they are well established.

As the organiser you will need to think about:

- providing child-sized tools for the children.
- storage and accessibility of tools.
- ensuring there is a nearby water supply.
- supervision of children while they are handling tools.

Planner: Planning daily visits to the wildlife garden will provide opportunities for different groups of children to observe change over time, in addition to finding and identifying a range of small creatures.

The joy in developing your wildlife-friendly garden lies in the unexpected; not knowing exactly what you might find when you go outside to look every morning. Look on this as a positive learning experience for everyone.

Key points

- Displaying interest in, and enthusiasm for, all that is happening in your setting will encourage the children to be involved, curious and questioning.
- As a communicator you will be actively listening as well as speaking, and
  encouraging the children to do the same.
- Skilful practitioners will be sensitive in the way in which they intervene in the children's discoveries.
- You will need careful organisation and management to create an environment which fosters curiosity and encourages exploration and investigation.
- Good planning underpins scientific teaching and learning and welcomes the
  unexpected.

Chapter 2

Supporting young children's curiosity

Curiosity is defined in the dictionary as 'an eager desire to know', and so is certainly a disposition which we would want to encourage in young children. Children's curiosity about the world around them is apparent from the moment they are born. As early years practitioners you will want to support and reinforce this innate curiosity to give children the confidence to develop their own theories about the world and how it works.

Fostering children's curiosity

The ethos of your setting, the attitudes of the adults working there and the way in which they talk with young children are central to encouraging children to be curious, confident, independent learners. Children's curiosity will thrive in an environment which recognises and values children's existing knowledge, ideas and experience.

In order to develop their confidence in exploration and investigation, it is important that children feel they can volunteer their ideas and share their experiences without fear of being ridiculed or told they are wrong. They need to feel secure in taking risks with their ideas in a safe, supportive environment.

Remember that children can display their curiosity in many different ways, not just through the questions they ask. Curiosity can be conveyed through body language, posture and stance, or through the length of time spent exploring an object or activity of interest, as well as by talking. For very young children curiosity tends to be impulsive as their attention is drawn to new and unusual objects and situations. As they become older, their curiosity is more focused as they pay more attention to detail and look for explanations for the things they see and experience.

Being a role model for curiosity is the best way adults can encourage children to be curious themselves. Being interested in everything going on in the world, and thinking out loud, is a great way to encourage the interest and involvement of those around you. Ask children open-ended questions that pose problems and encourage investigation, for example:

'I wonder what would happen if ...?' or 'How can I ...?'

Encourage children to ask questions themselves, and put forward their ideas and theories. Listen to children's responses and then plan activities on the basis of the responses they make.

As children become involved in investigating and exploring, you will find that they will often become totally absorbed and concentrate for long periods of time. Sometimes they will want to revisit a particular activity many times while they review and consolidate their understanding.

Think about how you can support children's curiosity by being flexible in your approach to the management of time, over a day, a week, or an extended period. This approach allows children to become involved in the long-term investigation of things of particular interest to them, for example growing vegetables or building a large-scale construction outdoors.

Environments for curiosity

Creating an environment for curiosity involves a range of different practical and management considerations, and you need to consider these in relation to the setting you work in.

- Provide interesting resources for the children which stimulate curiosity and invite exploration. These don't need to be elaborate or expensive, and they can be found all around you, indoors and out. Open your eyes and look for the extraordinary in the ordinary, the unusual in the usual.

- Invest in the best quality tools and resources you can afford, for example magnifiers, mirrors and magnets, to help children develop their skills of investigation and observation.

- Think about all the many different ways you could use mirrors and light to help children, and yourself, to see things differently.

- Remember the importance of using the outdoor as well as the indoor area in your setting. Think about the curiosity value of a spider's web covered in dew, snails hiding in a gap in the wall, a puddle and a shadow (see Chapter 8).

- Give the children time and space to satisfy their curiosity on large scale activities, for example outdoor construction, making musical instruments or digging and growing vegetables, which need space and could extend over several weeks.

- Build up a library of illustrated reference books, photographs, videos and CD-ROMs to support children in their enquiries. Remember that your local library will probably have a group-lending scheme.

- Demonstrate how you value children's curiosity and exploration by taking photographs and encouraging the children to make drawings and models to represent their ideas. Write down the words they use when talking about their discoveries and then use all this information to create an attractive, interactive display (see Chapter 6).

- Create opportunities for children to think, talk and listen, reflecting on what they have done, sharing ideas and observations with their friends, and learning to listen to the ideas and observations put forward by others (see Chapter 3).

Ideas for encouraging children's curiosity

Investigating shadows

Choose a sunny day, in either winter or summer, to go outside and explore shadows. Try going on a shadow hunt around your outdoor area.

- Where can you see shadows?
- What colour are they? Are they all the same colour?
- Do you think everything has a shadow?
- Who has the biggest shadow? Who has the smallest shadow?
- Can I escape from my shadow?
- Can you find some shadows which move and some which stand still?
- Can I cover my shadow up?
- Where do you think shadows come from?

Using some long lengths of paper you could encourage the children to help one another to draw around the outlines of their own shadows. Take these shadows back inside and compare their shapes and sizes. Take some photographs of shadows, including the shadow of the same object taken at different times of day.

Talk to the children about the different discoveries they have made about shadows and write down the comments they make. Help them to make a shadow display demonstrating all their different shadow investigations. Don't forget to include the children's many ideas and theories.

Investigating shadows in this way will encourage children to be observant and curious about the world around them. It will build up their overall experience of shadows and give them lots of ideas to think about as, over time, they deepen their understanding of how shadows are formed.

There are, of course, lots of opportunities to develop and extend this activity by playing with light and looking at shadows indoors.

How things work

Looking closely at kitchen tools provides lots of opportunities for children to investigate their shape, size, texture, materials, design and function.

Put together a collection of kitchen tools, which could include:

- spoons of different sizes, made of different materials, such as wood, metal and plastic. Include spoons with holes in and those with an unusual shape, such as ladles and honey spoons

- chopsticks, tongs, sieves and colanders
- potato masher, garlic press and a whisk.

Encourage children to investigate the tools carefully:

- What do they think they are made of? Look out for reflections in shiny metal spoons.
- What do they think they are for? See what interesting ideas the children come up with.
- How do they think they work? Some tools have simple levers and mechanisms which the children can investigate.
- Try providing some pots of rice, peas or sand and encourage the children to investigate which tools are best for separating and sorting mixtures. Some children will spend hours transferring individual grains of rice with chopsticks or small tongs.

Investigating how simple everyday things work helps children to develop their first-hand experience of the world. There will be lots of opportunities for them to extend their understanding when they are involved in different cooking activities, either in the setting or at home.

Key points

- Children's curiosity will thrive in an environment which values their existing knowledge, skills and experience.
- Curiosity can be displayed in many ways, not just through questions.
- Being a role model for curiosity is the best way to encourage children to be curious themselves.
- Demonstrate how you value children's curiosity and exploration by taking photographs and encouraging the children to make drawings and models to represent their ideas.
- Give children time and space to explore and investigate on a large scale.

Chapter 3

Creativity in science and technology

Traditionally, we associate creativity with the visual and expressive arts such as sculpture, painting, music and dance. However, if we pause to think of some of the most creative thinkers in the past and present, for example, Leonardo da Vinci, Stephen Hawking, Vivienne Westwood and James Dyson, it is clear that creativity is equally abundant, and as important, in the fields of science and design technology.

Bill Lucas, former director of the Campaign for Learning, defines creativity as:

'A state of mind in which all our intelligences are working together. It involves seeing, thinking and innovating and can be demonstrated in any subject or any aspect of life.'

If we adopt this version of creativity as our own, then we are acknowledging that everyone is creative in some way or another. Indeed, as Bernadette Duffy (1998) states:

'Creativity is about connecting the previously unconnected in ways that are meaningful to the individual.'

Providing opportunities for children to express their creativity through science and technology means giving them the opportunities to:

- express their ideas and theories
- make choices
- investigate the properties of materials and their potential
- make associations and connections
- experience the joy and satisfaction of discovering something new for themselves.

Children's ideas and theories

Young children frequently have very definite theories about how the world works, and it is well worth investing the time needed to explore their thinking and ideas. These theories are ideal starting points for exploration and investigation because they arise directly from the children's own interests and first-hand experience.

Plan time to have in-depth conversations with children about their ideas and what they believe to be true. Trust them to come up with interesting suggestions for things they would like to investigate and take these ideas seriously. You will find that children's theories will be very creative and may not always be those that are accepted by adults; they do, however, have their own value because they make sense to them at the time.

Making choices

Providing real choice for children affects all aspects of the organisation of your setting – the ethos, the layout of the environment and resources, the structure of the day and, above all, the confidence and attitudes of the staff.

In order to foster creativity in science and design technology, it is essential to offer children real choices so that they become confident in:

- making decisions on what to investigate, or to design and make
- choosing who to work with
- selecting resources
- finding a suitable space
- planning their time.

Investigating the properties of materials

From the very earliest age, children investigate the materials which they find around them, their food, their toys, their clothes and their environment, both indoors and out.

Understanding the properties of materials can only come from first-hand experience of what they feel like and how they behave. You will need to provide lots of opportunities for the children to explore a variety of materials for example, sand, water, clay, wood, metal and plastic, so that they become familiar with what materials can and can't do.

Are materials:

- soft or hard?
- rough or smooth?
- warm or cold?
- liquid or solid?
- weak or strong?
- malleable or rigid?
- transparent or opaque?

What happens if they are:

- stretched?
- squashed?
- twisted?
- heated?
- cooled?
- joined?

As children gain experience of handling and manipulating materials by playing with them, they will use their knowledge of the properties of materials creatively in scientific investigations and in designing and making.

Making associations and connections

Children are thinking creatively when they transfer their knowledge and understanding from one context to another. The day-to-day experience of playing with sand and adding water to it will lead to an understanding of how solids change when water is added to them. A child choosing to use this knowledge when investigating flour and water demonstrates clear associations between different areas of learning. The creative scientist will then investigate the effects of adding water to other solids such as clay, instant mashed potato, cornflour or sugar.

Experiencing the joy of discovery

As young children explore and investigate the world around them, they will experience the joy of discovering things for the first time. It is this awe and wonder about the world around them that will encourage their ongoing creativity and curiosity.

Children invest a great deal of emotion and feeling in the thinking which goes into their ideas and theories. Their comments and observations can be very profound at times and demonstrate deep thinking of a spiritual nature.

Although as adults we may be familiar with the world around us, we must remember to value the element of surprise and the excitement of not knowing exactly what will happen next. Enthusiastic, creative adults are the key to creative, enthusiastic children.

Ideas for exploring creativity

Creating with light – interacting with an overhead projector

Set up an overhead projector so that it projects across an area where the children can use construction materials. Place a screen behind the area where the children will build.

- Provide an interesting range of resources to use with the overhead projector. Make sure the resources are well organised and available next to the projector. You could include leaves, feathers, grasses, seed pods, shells and coloured acetate. Encourage the children to add to these.
- Talk to the children about how they will use the resources available to them to create an imaginary world. This will involve them in sharing space, resources and ideas.
- Ask the children questions. What do you think we could build? What would happen if we put some shells or leaves on the projector? Can we change the colour?
- Give the children time to investigate the different effects they can produce by :
  - building and constructing
  - changing, and adding to, the materials
  - introducing other resources into the area.

Use the opportunities that arise to draw the children's attention to the size and scale of the projected images and to the transparency and opacity of different materials. Some of the projected images will be dramatic and worth capturing in photographs. These will demonstrate the children's creativity and imagination, and their use of ICT. Talking to the children about the photographs will provide evidence of their scientific and technological understanding.

Sound pictures

Making connections using the different senses provides an interesting insight into children's creative thinking and expression. When investigating sound and musical instruments, try different ways of recording the experience.

- Provide a range of different instruments such as a drum, triangle, castanets, whistle or guitar.
- Make available a selection of paper, pencils and fine pens in a range of colours from pastel to primary shades.
- Investigate the sounds made by the different instruments – high, low, soft, loud, long, short, fast, slow – and talk about how the sounds are made.

- Play one of the instruments and ask the children to listen carefully to it.
- Ask them to choose the paper and pens or pencils they want to use to record the sounds made by the first instrument.
- Repeat the process with different instruments. Remember they may want to choose different coloured paper and pens for each instrument.
- Talk with them about how they have responded to and recorded the different sounds – colour, thickness of line, pattern and intensity of the mark-making.
- Try repeating the process with different recorded music – a march, a lullaby or a rap.

Using sound pictures enhances and enriches the exploration of sound by focusing on listening attentively. It provides opportunities to develop sound vocabulary and encourages the children to represent their scientific ideas creatively.

Key points

- Children's ideas and theories make ideal starting points for creative exploration and investigation.
- To develop creativity in science and technology children need opportunities to make real choices.
- It is only through understanding the properties of materials that children can use them creatively.
- Creative thinking is demonstrated by transferring knowledge and understanding from one context to another.
- Enthusiastic, creative adults are the key to creative enthusiastic children.

Chapter 4

Developing communication skills

Communication, in its broadest sense, is a fundamental aspect of human development which enables us to make sense of the world. Through communicating ideas, children are able to display their curiosity and express their creativity. The science and technology aspects of knowledge and understanding of the world present the perfect opportunity to develop communication skills, starting from the ideas that children have about their world and how it works. In their early years, children have a naturally investigative style of learning and an equally natural urge to communicate what they are doing and what they are discovering.

Communicating science

Although our image of science is about doing things, it is, in fact, far more about communicating our theories to ourselves and to others. This is clear when we look at the processes of science, which are:

- observing
- raising questions
- hypothesising
- predicting
- planning and carrying out an investigation or exploration
- interpreting results
- sharing findings.

During their scientific exploration there are many opportunities for children to develop a range of oral communication skills. They will experiment with language, learn how to explain, question, hypothesise and predict, as well as influence and persuade others of their arguments.

Scientific discovery at every level, from the Nobel Prize winner to the toddler investigating spaghetti hoops, has to be shared in order to be validated and of use to society. Scientists need the acknowledgement of their peers to validate that what they have discovered is true for the time being.

Communicating design and technology

Design technology is all about designing and communicating ideas. During the design process, children should be encouraged to look beyond their first thoughts to find better alternatives which will help them influence and control their environment.

The processes of design technology are:

- identifying a need or problem
- proposing solutions
- realising the design – making something
- evaluation and testing.

You will see that there are many opportunities to develop a range of communication skills during this process. Very often, a design technology activity is a shared experience where children make individual decisions and learn to appreciate feedback from their group. They will begin to appreciate the need for giving clear and accurate explanations, start to use specialist vocabulary and learn the value of working drawings. Their communication will be oral, graphic and mathematical and will include action as well as words.

Languages for communication

All inventors and designers need to share their progress and achievements with others. Their ideas can be communicated in many ways, for example through speaking, drawing, writing, constructing, music and dance, each of which has particular value in different situations.

Speaking and listening

Every group of children will have its scientific experts (machine lovers, gardeners, builders, plumbers, naturalists, inventors and cooks), who will have knowledge, skills and experience to communicate. When you value this range of expertise and create opportunities for ideas and opinions to be shared, you will help children to develop skills to communicate scientific ideas effectively. To do this they need to learn to:

- express their ideas with clarity
- take turns in discussion
- listen to other points of view
- be prepared to negotiate.

Science and technology activities will involve the use of different materials, equipment and processes, and you can use them as opportunities to introduce new and interesting vocabulary. Using new grown-up words, such as pneumatic, hydraulic, friction, gravity and equilibrium, can be a source of fascination.

Drawing and writing

Drawing conveys meaning and can be used as a tool to initiate, develop and communicate ideas. Some children who find using words difficult can express their ideas and reveal their thinking through drawing. All children will benefit from the challenge of conveying their thinking through graphic representation, using pictures, plans, maps and diagrams. When children represent their mental images in drawings they are also re-presenting the images to themselves, modifying their ideas and developing reasoning skills. Explaining their drawings to a group provides a further opportunity to revisit, revise and enrich their own understanding.

As they investigate, children will begin to use mark-making and writing skills. You can capitalise on this by providing opportunities to use labels, sequence events and write instructions. Group involvement in science and design technology will often lead to a consensus report of events and discoveries that will need the assistance of an adult.

Modelling and re-enactment

Some children may prefer to express their design ideas and scientific theories through models, construction, music, dance and re-enactment. Remember to recognise and value the wide range of forms of communication which young children use.

Ideas for stimulating communication

Exploring light and dark

This is a good winter investigation, when the mornings and evenings are dark.

- Make a collection of photographs and pictures illustrating day and night scenes.
- Have a discussion with the children about what happens when it is light and what happens when it is dark.
- To involve all children, remember to use open ended questions such as 'What do you think happens when ...?' and 'Do you remember ...?'.
- Listen to children's ideas and feelings about light and dark.
- Go outside at different times of day, early in the morning and late in the afternoon. Encourage the children to talk about the experience.

- What words can they invent to describe the different moods created by different light levels?
- Is it easier to see things on a bright sunny day or on a dull cloudy day?
- Do we have to be able to see our friends' faces clearly in order to recognise them? What other clues do we use?

Provide blankets, cardboard and a groundsheet for the children to use to make a den outside.

- Help them to plan how they will make the den. Can they predict what it will feel like inside?
- Having constructed the den, encourage them to describe how it feels inside. Is it warm, cold, light, dark, safe or scary?
- How could they light up the inside of the den?
- Will it keep them safe from dinosaurs?

Keeping teddy dry

This is a good design technology project which involves the different stages of planning, designing, making, evaluating and testing.

- Collect together a range of different raincoats, rain hats and umbrellas.
- Include pictures and photographs of rainwear; try to find some unusual examples of people (and animals) protecting themselves from the rain.
- Ask the children to bring in a teddy from home.
- Provide a range of resources for making a raincoat, hat or umbrella for teddy, for example plastic sheeting, fabric, paper, card, joining materials and fastenings, and the appropriate tools.
- Have a discussion with the children about why we want to

protect ourselves from the rain.
- Look at the range of different rainwear and ask the children to make judgements about:
  - which they like best and why
  - who might wear them
  - which they think would be best for keeping out the rain.
- Ask the children to design a rain cover for their teddy.
- Encourage them to make several drawings before choosing the one they want to make. A group of children may want to work together on this project.
- Using their own designs, support the children as they make their rain covers for their teddies.
- Talk about how you will test them to see which one works the best.
- Can they think of ways in which they might improve on their designs in the future?

Key points

- Young children have a naturally investigative style of learning and an equally natural urge to communicate.
- Children develop a range of oral communication skills during the process of scientific exploration.
- Design technology activity is often a shared experience, where children make individual decisions and learn to appreciate feedback from their group.
- Ideas can be communicated in many ways, for example, through speaking, drawing, writing, constructing, music and dance.
- All children will benefit from the challenge of conveying their thinking through graphic representation, using pictures, plans, maps and diagrams.

Chapter 5

Documenting thinking and learning

As we live in a technological world, building firm foundations for children's later scientific and technological understanding is as important as supporting their learning in numeracy and literacy. Their investigations and inventions do not necessarily produce an end product which can be appreciated and evaluated, so we must find ways of documenting children's ideas, theories and learning processes.

Listening carefully to children's theories, recording the exact words they use to describe their ideas and thoughts, and encouraging them to express their ideas in drawings and pictures will all help you to capture their learning processes.

What is documentation?

Documentation is not simply a collection of pictures and photographs put together at the end of an activity. Instead, it is a record of the process of children's learning (either individually or in groups) as they explore and investigate the world around them. Documentation involves the use of a range of visual and verbal records including:

- written transcripts and tape recordings of children's conversations and comments
- photographs and video recordings
- diaries
- children's drawings and paintings
- 3-D models and constructions.

Documentation is an integral part of scientific teaching and learning. It allows us to track children's learning experiences and gives us an insight into how children have reviewed and clarified their thoughts.

When children are involved in a scientific exploration they are engaged in the processes of science described in the previous chapter. These processes – observing, raising questions, hypothesising, predicting, planning and carrying out an exploration, interpreting results and sharing findings – are common to all scientific investigations and are best

demonstrated using different forms of documentation. For
example:

- When investigating a flower such as a poppy, children will
  have the opportunity to observe using all their senses.
  They will explore what it looks like, what it feels like, what it
  smells like and perhaps even what it sounds like.
- To document all these different learning experiences you
  may want to use photographs, drawings, paintings, 3-D
  models and a tape recording of children's comments and
  conversations.
- Capturing children's ideas and theories while they are
  hypothesising and predicting what will happen when
  vegetables of different types and sizes are rolled down
  a slope might involve using a tape recorder and written
  notes of their discussions and conversations.
- Documenting the planning, and carrying out an investigation
  such as growing cress would include photographs taken over
  a period of time, drawings, diaries and written commentaries.
- The final stages of the investigative process – interpreting
  results and sharing findings – involve disseminating
  information to a larger group. This might include other
  children in the setting, children in different classes, other
  practitioners, parents or carers and the wider community.
- Documentation in the form of words, photographs,
  drawings and 3-D representations provides the ideal
  medium for doing this.

How to document

You will need to think carefully about how you will
document. When documenting children's conversations, you

may find it difficult to be involved in the conversation, listen, and record all at the same time. Having another adult present would be helpful. If you decide to use a tape recorder, spend some time listening to and transcribing the conversation as soon as possible afterwards. Remember that it is important to capture the exact words the children use as they talk about their ideas and discoveries.

Photographs and video recordings provide a great deal of valuable information. Have a camera available at all times and remember to try to be inconspicuous when taking photographs and video. Organise a photo filing system from the outset and take time to process, label and file your photographs regularly. Match the photographs up with the children's comments and transcripts of their conversations along with any drawings, pictures or models they have created.

Why document?

Documentation is a way of making children's learning visible and can be used for a range of purposes by a variety of different audiences, for example other children, practitioners, families and the wider community. It also shows the children that you value their work.

Children

All children can benefit from the chance to revisit a discussion, perhaps by replaying a tape recording, in order to hear what they said as well as what was said by others. This will help them to make connections in their learning and to see how an idea or theory developed.

Photographs can capture the events, encounters, interactions and stages in an investigation or exploration. Revisiting these photographs allows children to reflect, re-evaluate and understand more clearly their earlier experiences, as well as giving them the opportunity to see how they themselves have made progress over time.

Producing and displaying a documentary record of a learning process gives children powerful positive messages about the value placed upon their ideas and discoveries.

Practitioners

Time spent reviewing the comments made by children, along with their drawings and photographs, will enable you to assess their progress and complete the foundation stage profile. It will also help you to plan effectively for the next stage of learning.

Documentation can be used during discussions with colleagues to gain a different perspective on your observations. Photographic records, particularly video footage, also help staff reflect on group interaction and group learning.

Families

Documentation can be shared with parents or carers to give them a wider understanding of their children's learning. Well-presented displays of documentation help families to understand the work of a setting. Starting from a natural interest in their individual child, parents will become increasingly involved in the progress of all of the children in your setting.

Wider community

High quality visual images can have an impact far beyond your setting. They can give a status and significance to children's learning within your community.

Documenting investigations and explorations

Light fantastic

A group of three- and four-year olds in an early years setting were investigating the magic of light and darkness. During a discussion about day and night the children's comments about light and dark, and their theories about where light comes from, were recorded by the practitioner. She also recorded the children's ideas and feelings about the dark – its excitement, scariness and dramatic qualities.

The children's interest in making light led to a simple investigation using electrical components. With just a bulb and a bicycle lamp battery the children explored ways of making the bulb light up. This activity took some time, but the practitioner resisted the urge to show the children what to do, and focused on recording their discussions instead.

When Meena successfully made her bulb light up, the practitioner asked her to explain to the rest of the group exactly how she had done it. There was then great excitement as all the children in the group were able to light up their bulbs. They then drew pictures of their circuits.

The practitioner was able to display the types of documentation which had been collected, including photographs of the circuit building activity and the successful outcomes, the drawings and models of the circuits and, crucially, the children's hypotheses and predictions about how lights work.

'Light fantastic' provided the opportunity to capture one of those elusive moments of awe and wonder which adults and children will enjoy revisiting at a later date.

The queen and the broad bean

Alice is a four year old child who recounts and records her investigations through story telling. With other children in her group she has been watching broad beans grow over a period of time.

Watching seeds germinate and start to grow is an exciting investigation which helps children to see the early stages of a plant life cycle. Once the beans have sprouted, they grow and change rapidly so there is something new to see every day, encouraging the children to look closely and revisit an activity regularly.

Alice chose to narrate the stages of her investigation through telling the story of 'The queen and the broad bean', which she wrote and illustrated in a drawing. The practitioner in the setting took photographs of the children watching the beans grow, helped them to produce a broad bean diary. She also captured Alice's story both in a photograph and as a transcript of the actual words she used in her story.

Designing and making without glue

In one nursery the practitioners decided that they would provide an opportunity for the children to design without glue to create a product which was ephemeral and open to the possibilities of change.

They were also interested in how groups of children, organised in terms of gender, would react to a shared activity which was open-ended in nature. Trays of coloured sand, fabric circles, and both reclaimed and natural materials were carefully laid out for the children to use. The practitioners set up a video camera to capture the interactions and dialogue as a group of boys worked on their communal design. Their chosen form of documentation allowed them to observe team planning and discussion, and to record the skills and dispositions, such as negotiation, co-operation, persistence and diligence, which the boys demonstrated.

Watching the video later, the practitioners were able to observe how individual members of the group were developing their fine motor skills and spatial awareness, making practical and aesthetic choices, putting forward their opinions, listening to others, and learning to adapt their ideas as necessary.

Each of these examples of choosing and using the different techniques of documentation provided the practitioners with evidence of the children's learning processes, which they then used to inform their future planning and to complete the foundation stage profile.

Key points

- Documentation is a record of the process of children's learning.
- Documentation involves the use of a range of verbal and visual records.
- It is important to capture the exact words that children use as they talk about their ideas and discoveries.
- Use documentation to make children's learning visible to a variety of audiences.
- Documentation is the key to planning the next stage in children's learning journeys.

Chapter 6

Displaying investigation and exploration

Traditionally, science and design and make activities rarely form the focus for displays in early years settings. We are more likely to see paintings, printing and pattern-making on the walls.

However, with a little thought, the documentation you have gathered (see Chapter 5) can be used to produce interesting and unusual interactive displays based around children's investigations and explorations. The display itself can actively contribute to effective learning and teaching and become the focus for new ideas and starting points.

While working with young children you will use many different strategies to share their learning with the children themselves, with colleagues and with parents or carers. High quality display will play a key role in helping you to do this, at the same time providing a very positive message about the value you place on children's ideas and thoughts.

Why do we use display?

Display has a number of important functions:

- information
- celebration
- interaction
- reflection.

Information

Displays provide information, in written and pictorial form, which describes the learning process to children, parents, carers, staff and visitors, including Ofsted inspectors.

Well-presented labels, transcripts of children's conversations, drawings, photographs and models can be used to explain how an investigation progressed, showing the starting point, questions raised, theories developed and evidence collected.

Celebration

Spending time and effort on documenting children's learning and displaying it with care and attention to detail, gives children very powerful messages about how you value their competence in exploration and investigation. Involving children in creating the display gives them a sense of ownership and the opportunity to celebrate their own personal achievements.

Interaction

Displays which focus on science and technology should pose questions and invite participation. If you include magnifiers, mirrors, construction materials or ICT equipment, such as an overhead projector, these will bring a display to life and lead to new starting points and questions to be investigated.

Reflection

Objects which may seem to be commonplace to adults, such as sunflowers, crystals, semi-precious stones, a leaf skeleton or a giant pine cone, can all provide moments of excitement and delight for young children. Including things of beauty, books, music and photographs will add an aesthetic dimension to children's discoveries about the world around them. Sensitive use of photography will capture moments of awe and wonder to add to the display.

Presenting science and technology displays

It is important to think about a number of aspects when creating science and design technology displays, such as the backgrounds, mounting, labelling and the use of 3-D.

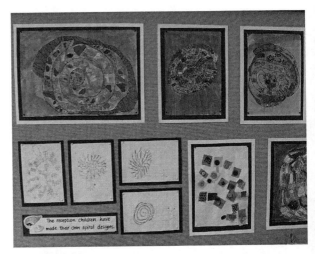

The reception children have made their own spiral designs.

Backgrounds

Backgrounds which use primary colours have a tendency to become the centre of attraction and detract from the purpose of the display.
Try using subtle-coloured backing papers, such as grey, cream, pastel shades, black or white. Textured papers and fabrics can be used as a background, or as drapes.

Carefully chosen borders can complement the background, but they need constant maintenance to prevent them becoming tatty.

Mounting

Careful attention should be paid to how a display is mounted; ideally the mounting fastenings should be invisible. Use clear mounting pins, a mini stapler opened out, Velcro, double-sided tape or a pin push. A heavy duty staple gun is rarely needed.

Double- or even triple-mounting of children's drawings and writing will show the value you place upon their efforts.

Labelling

Understanding the importance of clear, well organised and accurately placed labels is part of children's scientific and technological learning. Labels should be well mounted and provide an opportunity to use the correct technical vocabulary.

3-Dimensional

Displays should not be limited to 2-D displays on walls. The investigative nature of science and technology calls out for interactive 3-D displays utilising tables, shelves and the floor. Shelves can be created on 2-D displays by fixing open boxes, or corex, using a pin push and straight pins.

Taller boxes or tubes can be used as plinths to display models or artefacts.

Try enhancing your display with:

- well-illustrated non-fiction books on bookstands
- natural and found materials
- good quality photographs
- objects of interest and beauty
- mirrors – both flat and curved
- an infinity box

- sound
- a question box
- a mini light box
- projected images using an overhead projector.

Using display to enhance your scientific activities

How things work

Children are fascinated from a very early age with machines and how they work. Ordinary kitchen tools provide many examples of very simple machines using levers, cogs and simple mechanisms.

This example shows how an interactive display, used as part of a topic on how things work, can be used to encourage children to work independently.

What you need:

- hand lenses and a stand magnifier
- a display of kitchen tools positioned at child height on a table
- clipboards, drawing paper and pencils.

What you do:

Set up your display of kitchen tools on a table. Try displaying a hand rotary whisk, garlic press or potato ricer, nutcrackers, tea strainer and pastry brush and crimper.

- Use a plain background for your display so the features of the tools are easy to see.
- Use book stands and clear plastic stands to display photographs and books, which illustrate tools and how they work.
- Include a magnifier and hand lens as part of the display so the children can look closely at the different tools and mechanisms independently.
- You could select a tool or mechanism to be the focus of the day by placing it under the stand magnifier and encouraging the children to look at the detail of the object.
- Some children will want to record their observations; make clipboards, paper and sharp pencils available next to the display.
- During whole group discussions encourage the children to talk about what they have observed.
- Create a wall display behind the table by mounting children's close observational drawings, comments and transcripts of group conversations.
- You could extend the children's interest in the display by adding a mirror or mirror tile to encourage children to look at the objects from unusual angles.
- Use the opportunity to introduce the correct technical vocabulary connected with the activity, for example, see, look, observe, notice, view, lens, magnifier, closely, detail, focus, tools, machines, levers, cogs, mechanism.

An ever changing display

Overhead projectors can be used in many different ways to support investigation and exploration. Children will really enjoy using an overhead projector to create ever changing displays on a clear wall in your setting or on a sheet suspended from the ceiling.

What you need:

- an overhead projector that does not heat up when left on for long periods. Older models are often best
- a safe place to set up the overhead projector, preferably next to a wall so there are no trailing leads. Set the projector up at the correct height for the children to use it easily
- a range of resources, natural and man-made, translucent and opaque, for the children to use.

What you do:

Encourage the children to investigate a wide range of objects and the shadows they make.
- Give the children time to discover what happens when different things are placed on the overhead projector screen. Try coins, buttons, glass nuggets, transparent sweet wrappers, feathers and leaf skeletons.

- Encourage the children to collaborate as they experiment with the display and to talk about the images and effects that are produced.
- Use this as an opportunity to involve the children in creating a striking, ever changing, display for their learning environment.

Key points

- Interesting and unusual interactive displays can be based around children's investigations and explorations.
- High quality display plays a key role in sharing children's learning.
- Good quality display gives children very powerful messages about how you value their competence in exploration and investigation.
- The investigative nature of science and technology calls out for interactive 3-D displays.
- Sensitive use of photography during an activity will capture those special moments of awe and wonder to add to a display.

Chapter 7

Science and technology in everyday life

Having an understanding of science enables us to make sense of the physical and biological world in which we live. From the day they are born, children are actively exploring their surroundings with all their senses and developing their own theories about how things work.

Science makes an important contribution to children's intellectual and social development and fosters their thinking and reasoning skills. For example, playing with shadows leads to enquiry into shape, size, position, opacity and transparency and gives children opportunities to make connections between light and materials.

Designing and making, or design technology, is an integral part of early childhood experience. As they acquire knowledge children begin to apply what they know to create new products and processes which influence their world. For example, when some children are working in the construction area they may use their knowledge of materials and forces to design and build a castle. Their design technology competence will then change the focus of their imaginary play.

Scientific knowledge

Scientific knowledge and understanding is divided into seven key areas:

- living things
- materials
- air, atmosphere and weather
- structure of the earth
- earth in space
- forces
- energy.

Traditionally, the study of living things has been popular in early years settings through topics such as 'all about me', 'my pets' and 'growing things'. However, many other opportunities are available for developing scientific knowledge and understanding.

- The properties of materials can be explored through construction, shadow-play and magnetism.
- Long-term observation of the seasons provides first-hand opportunities to learn about air, atmosphere and weather.
- Investigating clay, sand, rocks, pebbles and going on visits to the beach facilitates early investigation of the structure of the earth.

- Experiencing night and day and being aware of the sun, stars and moon through stories, rhymes and actual experience will stimulate interest in the earth in space.
- Objects which roll, stretch, and move by pushing, pulling or twisting will all provide opportunities for children to experience the effects of forces.
- A collection of toys which move using wind or water power or electricity will stimulate discussion about types of energy.

Design technology

Knowledge and understanding within design technology includes:

- materials
- energy

- structures
- control.

- Designing and making an umbrella or sunshade for teddy will lead to an investigation of the properties of materials: which are waterproof, which will fold, which are strong and which will tear.
- Looking at many different types of windmills, in the countryside, at the beach or in the garden centre will encourage the children to see how wind provides energy to make things move.
- Building a bridge for the Billy Goats Gruff will lead to an understanding of structures, stability, strength and ways of joining things.
- Programmable toys, such as Roamer, lay the foundation for young children's understanding of control technology.

Developing skills

Scientific exploration and investigation is an ideal way to develop a range of practical skills including close observation, measuring and counting, early mark-making and pictorial representation. When designing and making, children will develop their manipulative skills and fine motor control as they refine their use of tools and materials.

In Chapter 4 the value of science and technology in developing communication skills is explored in detail. Children will experiment with language, learn how to explain, question, hypothesise and predict as well as influence and persuade others of their arguments.

There are many opportunities for social skills to be developed through group interaction in scientific and technological exploration. Children will learn to have their opinions and listen to those of others, to negotiate, co-operate and value the contributions of others.

Scientific investigation encourages children to develop the thinking and reasoning skills of hypothesising, developing theories, predicting and making connections between areas of knowledge.

Remember that, in solving a design technology problem children will begin to use a whole range of planning, evaluation and research skills.

Dispositions and feelings

First hand experiences, working as part of a group and the opportunity to make choices and express ideas will help children to develop the long term attitudes, or dispositions, for learning.

Involvement in scientific exploration, and designing and making, fosters individual children's curiosity, creativity, self confidence, open mindedness, critical reflection, motivation, initiative, enthusiasm, persistence and diligence.

Group activity will develop co-operation, leadership, empathy, generosity and helpfulness. Children will have the opportunity to feel self-confident, self-controlled, secure, accepted and fulfilled.

Using everyday experiences

Here are some examples of everyday activities which can
be a starting point for real scientific and technological
exploration. These will all help to develop knowledge, skills
and dispositions.

Water tray

- physical properties of water – transparency, fluidity
- things which float and sink
- the effect of water on other materials - dissolving, absorbency
- water power – waterwheels and hydraulics
- measuring volume and capacity.

Sand tray

- physical properties of a material composed of particles
- relationship between natural materials, eg. shells, stones
  and sand
- sieving and separating mixtures
- properties and uses of wet and dry sand
- use of tools and simple machines.

Construction area

- properties of materials, eg. wood, plastic, paper, rubber
- stability – building towers and bridges
- forces – making things move
- making plans and designs
- joining materials
- using appropriate tools and equipment safely.

Cooking

- liquids and solids – melting and freezing
- hot and cold – cooking and cooling
- wet and dry
- mixing and separating – sieving and sifting
- smelling and tasting
- how kitchen tools work – levers, rolling, squashing, cutting
- healthy eating.

This presents a good opportunity to talk to the children about 'staying safe' – washing our hands before handling food, using sharp knives carefully, not touching hot surfaces and being aware that some children can have allergic reactions to certain foods.

Role Play area - garden centre

- sorting and classifying - garden tools and flowerpots
- planting seeds and watching them grow
- forces and simple machines – lifting and shifting
- close observation – plants, leaves, cones and seeds
- designing and making plant labels and packaging.

Music making

- listening to rhythm and pitch of sounds

- investigating how far sound can travel
- identifying different sounds in the environment
- making musical instruments – shakers, drums, pipes, castanets, bells
- recording sounds using ICT.

Outdoors

- investigating habitats – in the log pile, under a stone
- observing living things
- investigating light and shadows
- using energy and keeping fit
- designing and making dens
- wet and dry – puddles and washing lines
- weather watching.

Science and technology are all around us in our everyday lives. It is important that we actively engage with the children in the many opportunities presented on a day-to-day basis.

We often see autumn leaves used for decorative purposes or to stimulate work with pattern and colour, but the scientific opportunities are lost. These same autumn leaves can be used as a basis for scientific investigation – to help children recognise similarities and differences, to identify types of trees, to investigate sound and materials and to begin to understand life processes.

Key points

- Science and technology are concerned with things in our surroundings which can be investigated with all our senses.

- Young children have an entitlement to experience the physical sciences as well as the living world.
- Practical, communication, social and reasoning and thinking skills are all developed through science and technology.
- First-hand experience, group working, making choices and expressing ideas help children to develop positive dispositions for learning.
- It is important that we actively engage with the children in the many scientific and technological opportunities presented on a day-to-day basis.

Chapter 8

Exploring collections

Collections of simple everyday objects provide excellent starting points for exploration and investigation. They are interesting to put together, inexpensive, and can be linked to a wide range of different themes and topics. In addition they make good use of open-ended resources which pose questions and encourage curiosity (see Chapter 2).

Planning a collection

You can use collections to support both the short- and long-term planning processes you have adopted in your setting. You may want your collection to be central to a science based topic, to support a theme or enrich children's everyday experiences.

Using collections in a science based topic

You may choose to plan for the following topics in a year:

Toys   Try using a collection of toys that move in different ways, or toys that make a noise.

Clothes   Make a collection of hats or shoes.

Food   Put together a collection of kitchen tools that
            shape, squash or measure.

Using collections in theme-based planning

Throughout the year some themes or strands of learning
regularly recur. Collections can be used to support themes
which are of particular interest to children, or which develop
specific scientific and technological skills and understanding.

For example:

Moving things   Make a collection of wheeled vehicles.
Colour   Create a collection of fabric and paper
                      samples or paint shade cards.
Sorting things   Use a collection of buttons which can be
                      sorted using several different
                      criteria.

Collections to enrich everyday experiences

Collections can be used to enrich the children's day-to-day
experiences by providing stimulating resources to engage
their attention and encourage curiosity and communication
(see Chapter 4). Used in this way, collections will fuel
children's imagination and creativity (see Chapter 3) and
enrich the quality of learning in day-to-day activities. As an
example, you could put together collections to support these
different activities in your setting.

Water and sand play   A collection of things with
                           holes.

Role play and storytelling   A collection of boxes, large and small.

Outdoor play   A collection of things that roll.

Putting your collection together

The variety of objects you will want to include in one of your collections will go beyond the range of everyday toys and equipment which are usually available to children in an early years setting.

When selecting items to include, you need to apply the same criteria as you would for any other resources used by the children. They should be clean, well-maintained and safe for children to handle.

Keep in mind the health and safety guidelines that apply to your setting. *Be Safe*, a publication of the Association for Science Education (ASE) is a very useful, up-to-date source of information for schools and early years settings.

Make sure that both children and adults are aware that the resources in the collection are something special, to be used in a particular way, and not toys for everyday use. Reinforcing this message will help to preserve the integrity of the collection you have worked so hard to assemble. It will also help to retain the interest and excitement which using the collection should invoke.

To help you build up your collection, you may find the following list of people and places useful. Depending on your local circumstances and the nature of the collection you are making, you will no doubt think of many others.

People who can help

- staff of the setting or school
- families, including older and more distant relatives
- committee members/governors
- local community and local businesses.

Places to visit

- charity shops, markets and car boot sales
- garden centres, kitchen and household shops
- builders' merchants
- the local park, country or seaside.

Putting together collections can become a useful focus for involving family members in the life of your setting. It can also provide an enjoyable way to encourage parents or carers in supporting their children's learning.

Using collections to engage in the processes of science

Collections of everyday things can be used as starting points for the whole process of scientific exploration and investigation (see Chapter 4).

For example, using a collection of leaves children can:

Observe	Look closely at shape, size, pattern and texture.
Raise questions	'Why are some leaves bigger than others?'

Hypothesise and predict	All tall trees have big leaves.
Investigate	Explore trees and investigate the size, arrangement, colour and texture of their leaves.
Interpret and share findings	Through talking, drawing, painting, photographs.

Putting together and investigating collections provide lots of different opportunities for children to develop their skills in close observation, using all their senses, not just their sense of sight. They can investigate the sound, smell and texture of objects, notice fine detail and develop their vocabulary as they describe similarities and differences.

Thinking of questions to ask encourages children to be curious and to begin to take responsibility for their own learning. While hypothesising and predicting, children are developing their ability to think logically, and through investigating and sharing their findings they learn to express their ideas and thoughts clearly and to listen to the ideas and theories of others.

Ideas for using collections

A collection of shoes

A shoe shop in the role-play area could contain a collection of shoes

- made from different materials: leather, plastic, fabric, rubber
- with different fastenings: laces, velcro, buckles, elastic

- of different sizes: baby shoes, large size adult shoes
- for different purposes: boots, trainers, flip flops
- with different soles: smooth leather, ridged rubber
- for particular purposes: ballet shoes, tap shoes, football boots, wellingtons.

Investigating the collection of shoes will provide lots of opportunities to look at the properties of materials, the use of different materials for different purposes, how materials are fixed together and how different types of fastenings work.

Storing the collection attractively, in shoe boxes of different sizes for example, will add enormously to its appeal and encourage children to treat it with respect. Putting photographs of the shoes on the front of the box will encourage recognition, matching and sorting.

A collection outdoors

Putting together a collection of 'joining things' for use outdoors will act as a starting point for a wide range of large scale design technology investigations.

The collection might include:

- rope, string, elastic, masking tape, parcel tape, garden wire, clothes pegs, zips, Velcro
- a range of construction materials such as: wood, plastic, fabrics and natural materials.

Fixing materials together while building dens, castles and caves is a very practical way to investigate the properties of materials and how simple tools work, the spring in a clothes peg for instance. The collection should be stored in a container which displays the different components attractively and is easily transportable.

Collections of natural materials

A collection of natural materials costs little or nothing to make and is a wonderful way of drawing children's attention to the wonders of the world around them. An attractive display will soon become an interesting feature of your setting, to be used and added to over time.

Your collection may start by reflecting your local area, comprising:

- leaves, grasses, twigs, bark, stones, feathers, seed pods and cones. These can be added to over time with interesting examples from further afield

- shells, sand, polished stones, skeleton leaves, oddly shaped roots and branches, giant seed pods, cones and dried fruits.

In addition to using the collection of natural materials to support children's understanding and skills in science and technology, it also provides a wonderful starting point for creative expression, mathematical and language development.

Key points

- Collections make good use of open ended resources which pose questions and encourage investigation and exploration.
- Collections can be central to a science-based topic, support a theme or enrich children's everyday experiences.
- Storing the collection attractively will add enormously to its appeal and will encourage children to treat it with respect.
- A collection of natural materials costs little or nothing to make and is a wonderful way of drawing children's attention to the wonders of the world around them.
- Putting together collections can become a useful focus for involving family members in the life of your setting. It is also an enjoyable way of encouraging parents or carers to support their children's learning.

Chapter 9

Making the most of outdoor spaces

The outdoor environment around your setting is a wonderful resource to use for investigation and exploration, not only for the plants and animals which make up the living world, but also for the houses, shops, roads and services that constitute the built environment.

Investigating and exploring outdoors

If children have the opportunity to explore and investigate outdoors, this will:

- develop their curiosity about the world around them, both natural and man-made, and acts as a powerful stimulus to keep their attention
- provide lots of opportunity for first-hand learning and discovery
- encourage them to observe carefully, using all their senses
- builds directly on their everyday experiences and encourage all children to contribute their observations, thoughts and ideas
- encourage children to be physically active and to enjoy and appreciate the outdoor environment.

Investigating the built environment

Children encounter the built environment every day, regardless of whether they live in a hamlet, a village, a town or large city. Investigating the built environment gives children real experiences of several aspects of science including forces, energy, materials and air, atmosphere and weather. It also provides examples of design technology using materials, energy, structures and control (see Chapter 7).

The built environment is made up of a wide range of places, services and people, including:

- buildings of different types, including houses, shops and public buildings such as schools, early education settings, libraries and places of worship
- networks of roads and railways
- signs and symbols, and examples of information communication technology, eg. traffic lights and street lighting
- services and utilities, such as water, drains and sewers, telephones, gas and electricity
- green spaces
- a rich variety of sounds, smells and textures
- the people who live and work in the built environment.

Remember, careful planning and preparation, in line with the setting's agreed policy framework, is an essential pre-requisite of a successful walk, journey or visit. Safety considerations are extremely important, but they should not prevent children experiencing the rich opportunities of the outside world.

Try some of these ideas as starting points for investigating the built environment around your setting.

Along the street

Before you set out:

- Gather together a collection of pictures of buildings from books, magazines and estate agents' literature.
- Talk with the children about the different types of buildings, and look for features they have in common such as walls, doors, windows and roofs.
- Look for the shapes and sizes of doors and windows, and patterns in brickwork and stone.

While you are out:

- Go out for a walk in your local neighbourhood along a route that includes examples of different types of buildings.
- Help the children to notice the different features of the buildings, and if possible take some photographs of the different buildings you see. Note down the comments made by the children when describing what they see, hear, feel and smell.
- Don't forget the importance of children investigating with all their senses: touching rough brick, bumpy pebbledash or smooth marble to experience different texture, smelling new paintwork or sawn timber, hearing the sounds of earth movers or cement mixers.

When you get back:

- Talk about the different buildings you have seen, what they look like, what they are made of, what they are used for.

- Using the photographs you have taken and any pictures the children have drawn, help them to reconstruct the story of their journey, including the comments they made while they were out.
- Some children may enjoy making 3-D representations of the buildings using clay, dough or construction materials.

Looking at lights

This works well in winter when there will be lots of different lights to look out for outside.

Before you set out:

- Look with the children at a collection of photographs of lights being used outside. These could include street lights, car headlights, floodlights, security lights, advertising signs and traffic lights.
- Have a discussion about what the different lights are for. For safety: street lights and car headlights. To give instructions: traffic lights. To attract attention: advertising signs and shop lights.
- Use this as an opportunity to talk about road safety and the importance of being seen clearly at night.

While you are out:

- Go out on a walk along a route that has examples of lots of different types of lights.
- See how many different types of lights the children can find on their walk.
- Spend some time looking at a set of traffic lights from a safe distance to observe the way they control the flow of the traffic.

When you get back:

- Talk about the different sorts of lights you experienced, where they were and what they were for.
- Help the children to make a dark den in a corner or under a table, where they can use torches and coloured acetate to see what happens when white light shines through a coloured filter.
- Look again at the photograph collection and talk about all the different activities that happen in the dark. What would happen if the lights went out?

Exploring the natural environment

Every setting will differ in the amount of outdoor space it has for children to access, and how this is designed and laid out. Even the smallest outdoor space can be developed into an interesting resource for studying plants and animals and for encouraging children to find out more about the natural world.

Over time this will help children to see the value of different types of environments and the importance of respecting and preserving them.

To help children explore the natural environment safely and effectively it is important to provide them with the appropriate resources. These would include:

- child sized trowels, buckets, spades and wheelbarrows
- boots and waterproof clothing
- plastic plant pots, compost, seed trays and planters

- seeds, bulbs, plants and cuttings
- bug viewers, magnifiers, hand lenses, Perry's pooters
- stand magnifiers and good quality drawing materials to encourage them to make close observational drawings
- materials for constructing bird feeders, houses and baths
- good quality, child sized binoculars
- reference books and sources. Use your local library.

Developing your natural environment

Creating a series of mini-environments over a period of time will bring a diverse range of plants and small animals into the area around your setting.

Flower and vegetable beds

Position these so the children can access them easily and can work on them without damaging surrounding plants and flowers. If you have the space you could use part of your garden area for this. Alternatively, try large, deep planters or barrels. These areas can be used for digging, raking, sowing, planting, weeding and harvesting, and also for attracting butterflies, bees, earthworms and ladybirds.

Setting up a log pile

The purpose of a log pile is to provide food, shelter and a place to breed for a wide range of small invertebrates. The ideal position for the log pile is a damp shady corner where the logs won't be accidentally disturbed. Keep the pile low so it doesn't present any danger to children.

The ideal starting material is a log that has already started to rot, to which you can add twigs, small branches and fallen leaves. The log pile will quickly become populated with all sorts of small creatures that you can observe by gently moving the logs and looking underneath. Some invertebrates can be removed temporarily so the children can look at them more closely, but make sure they are returned to the pile again when they have finished looking at them.

Bird feeders

Setting up bird feeders will soon attract a range of different species of birds to visit your setting, each with it own particular food preference and mode of feeding.

- Bird tables are good for seed mixes, fat, grated cheese, mealworms and soaked dried fruit.

- Hanging feeders can be filled with peanuts or sunflower seeds, and you can also hang up fat balls and cakes.
- Berry-bearing bushes and trees, eg. rowan, cotoneaster and holly, will all attract birds into your garden area.

Remember to provide a supply of fresh drinking water every day, and don't be surprised if the birds decide to have a bath in it.

Key points

- Exploring the outdoor environment develops young children's curiosity about the world around them, both natural and man-made, and acts as a powerful stimulus to keep their attention.
- The built environment is made up of a wide range of places, services and people.
- Even the smallest outdoor space can be developed into an interesting resource for study and for encouraging children to find out more about the natural world.
- Safety considerations are extremely important, but they should not prevent children experiencing the rich opportunities of the outside world.

Chapter 10

Involving families

In the previous chapters we have looked at a range of ways in which you and your colleagues in your setting can use exploration and investigation to encourage young children's curiosity and creativity and to help them communicate their ideas. In this chapter we highlight the important part which families play in working with you to develop these essential skills and dispositions.

Parents and carers can do much to foster curiosity, creativity and communication in their children, both by giving encouragement and by organising activities that will fascinate young minds.

From the day they are born, children are actively trying to make sense of the world around them. They are supported in their journey of discovery by the significant adults who surround them at this early age, parents, carers and their wider family – the child's first educators. Your setting has a crucial role to play in valuing the contribution families make to their children's scientific and technological learning, both now and in the future.

Supporting children's learning at home

First and foremost, parents, carers and family members should be aware of the importance and value you place on their continuing involvement in their child's learning. To work effectively with families in supporting their children as inventors and investigators you need to:

- share the philosophy of your setting with parents and value the role that parents and carers play as the child's first educator
- support parents and carers in developing an understanding of the inquisitive child to ensure that children receive consistent messages which encourage them to ask questions and have good ideas
- help parents and carers to see the importance of making time at home for opportunities and experiences which will develop their child's scientific interest
- demonstrate how everyday things, found around the

house, garden and in the local area, can become a source of curiosity to young children

- talk about the importance of letting children take risks and make mistakes.

Risky freedom involves creating an environment where children can try things out and find out 'what happens if...'. This could refer to either physical risk or to children feeling confident to take risks with their ideas. Managing physical risky freedom requires practitioners to carry out a thorough risk assessment. They should then plan carefully to see how they can provide appropriate opportunities and experiences for children in a well-organised manner. Helping children to feel confident to take risks with their ideas involves developing their self-esteem and self-confidence, encouraging them to come up with ideas and listening carefully to what they have to say.

Many adults are intimidated by science and technology and may not feel confident in their ability to support young children in this area of learning.

To help parents or carers overcome this you can:

- Encourage family members to act as role models by expressing their curiosity in the world around them.

- Make sure parents or carers know that they do not need to know all the answers to their children's questions, and that it is far better to look for the answers together.
- Underline the value of listening to children and paying attention to their ideas and theories.
- Explain how important it is to give children time; time to talk and listen, to play, to investigate and learn together and, most important of all, to have fun.

A few things to think about

- Are families encouraged to become involved with the children's projects and scientific activities?
- How are parents or carers helped to find out more about how young children learn?
- Can parents access a library of activities, resources

and bright ideas to help them extend their children's exploration and investigation at home?

Developing parents' and carers' understanding of science and technology

Have you thought about organising 'learning together' activities on themes such as exploration, investigation and discovery? Early years and childcare settings are ideally placed to build the confidence of parents and family members through the relationships of trust and mutual respect which develop around the care and education of a young child (Brunton and Thornton, 2006).

For many parents or carers the setting will represent their first opportunity for some considerable time to re-engage with a learning environment. A learning together event can act as something of a watershed, a time to consider re-entering the world of work or a stimulus for parents or carers to address their own learning needs in order to be able to fully support their child's ongoing education.

The science and technology projects, activities, visits and outings which young children in your setting are involved in can also act as powerful learning situations for parents and family members, and often extend their range of experiences as well those of the children.

Family workshops, with adults and children playing and learning together, are an ideal, non threatening way to open up the possibilities for parents and carers to extend their learning and accessing new skills. Some parents may use this as a gateway to accredited family learning programmes and then move on to focused skills development programmes. Workshops that focus on science and technology often appeal to male family members, who feel comfortable in sharing their expertise with their young children.

Ideas for parents to try at home

Suggest that parents try some of the following activities with their children:

- Watch and feel what happens when you create unusual mixtures, such as jelly and mashed potato, shaving foam and glitter, leaves and soil.
- Look at and talk about kitchen tools with your children. Can they guess the purpose of the tools and how they work?
- Use cardboard boxes and material to build a den. Explore what it is like inside.
- Investigate melting by placing some ice cubes in a warm place and watching what happens as you play with them.
- Gather together a selection of smelly objects. Cover them or close your eyes and play a guessing game to try and identify them.
- Observe the colours, shapes and patterns of plants in pots, in the garden or in the park.
- Set up a bird feeder where you can see it. Put out different types of food and wait to see which kinds of birds are attracted to them.
- Take your children outside in the early morning or evening to experience a sunrise or sunset.

- Go out for a walk in the winter on a clear winter's night to look at the stars and the moon.
- Shine a torch or a lamp against a wall and use your hands to make shadow shapes of birds, insects, animals and monsters.

Curiosity boxes

Why not set up a lending library of curiosity boxes for families to borrow. You could make the following boxes for families to use to encourage their children's curiosity, exploration and investigation at home.

- Close up: magnifying glass, bug viewer, fine pencils or pens
- Collect it: containers with lids, net or sieve, trowel
- Make it work: dough, found (recycled) materials and construction sets
- Moving water: funnel, tubing and containers of different sizes.
- Light and dark: torch, resources to make a den, shadow puppets.

Key points

- Value parents, carers and families as the child's first educators.
- The quality of the partnership which you establish with parents or carers will have long lasting effects on their attitudes to learning about science and technology.
- Reassure parents that they do not need to know all the answers to children's questions. It's far better to find out together.

- Reinforce the importance of family members as role models, expressing their interest and curiosity in the world around them
- Workshops which focus on science and technology often appeal to male family members who feel comfortable in sharing their expertise with their young children.

Chapter 11

Science and citizenship

The notion of young children as citizens is not one which practitioners will immediately associate with the foundation stage. However, when we consider what citizenship, or being a good citizen, actually means in relation to young children, it is very easy to see how important the early years are in laying the foundations for the future.

For a young child this means developing self-awareness and self-confidence, learning how to play and work well with others and recognising his or her place in the wider community. Exploration and investigation in science and design technology provide an ideal context in which to foster the dispositions and attitudes that are the essential attributes of a good citizen.

Laying the foundations

In Key Stage 1 citizenship is part of the broader framework of personal, social and health education (PSHE) and citizenship. This framework aims to give pupils the knowledge, skills and understanding they need to lead confident, healthy, independent lives and to become informed, active, responsible citizens.

This builds directly on young children's experience in the foundation stage where the early learning goals identify the following aspects of learning which underpin citizenship:

- dispositions and attitudes
- self-confidence and self-esteem
- making relationships
- behaviour and self control
- language for communication
- language for thinking
- exploration and investigation.

Growing good citizens

Citizenship involves taking responsibility for oneself, others and the environment. In the earlier chapters in this book we have given examples of science and design activities in the foundation stage which provide opportunities for children to develop these responsibilities:

Responsibility to self includes being curious, making choices and understanding safety and rules. It also involves learning to be persistent and diligent and being prepared to demonstrate leadership skills.

Responsibility to others means learning to explore and investigate with others, making friends and building relationships. It involves understanding rules, taking turns and cooperating.

Responsibility to the environment includes making decisions, selecting resources and taking care of the built and natural environment.

An environment for citizenship through science

An environment for citizenship through science is one that helps children to be independent and self-reliant by encouraging them to:

- make choices
- express ideas
- discuss and negotiate
- listen to different points of view
- be open minded and reflective.

Many opportunities to foster the skills, dispositions and attitudes which help children develop as responsible young citizens occur through exploration and investigation in your setting. Careful planning will help you make the most of these opportunities and maximise the learning opportunities they provide.

When planning for science and design technology, think about:

- how you encourage children to form opinions and to respect the opinions of others

- the expectations you have of children's interactions with one another, and with adults
- the way individual and group activities are organised to encourage cooperation, teamwork and leadership
- how the indoor and outdoor spaces and resources are organised
- ways to make sure the children have time to follow through their investigations.

Ideas for fostering citizenship

Try using the explorations described below as opportunities to foster young children's citizenship through science and design technology.

Guess whose shadow

Early Learning Goals for:

- personal, social and emotional development (PSED): making relationships
- knowledge and understanding of the world (KUW): exploration and investigation.

As adults, you will be very familiar with shadows, but remember that many children will be experiencing this excitement and wonder for the first time. This activity is a good opportunity to help the group of children to negotiate the rules for a game.

- Secretly put together a collection of everyday objects which you think will make interesting shadows. You might choose a

large key, a model dinosaur, a pair of scissors or a hat.
- Choose a dark place in your setting. You could draw the blinds or use screens or drapes to block out the light. You also need a strong torch and a space for the children to sit facing a blank space on the wall.
- Tell the children that you are going to play a game called, 'Guess whose shadow?', and that to play the game they have to follow the instructions carefully.
- Help them to understand that the game will only work if they sit facing the wall and do not turn around when the torch is switched on. Explain that one person will act as the 'shadow maker' and the others have to guess whose shadow it is. Help them to understand that they will each be able to have a turn at being the 'shadow maker'.
- Ask the children to sit facing the wall, then switch on the torch and turn out the lights.
- Stand behind the children and shine the torch on the wall.
- Hold an object in front of the torch so that its shadow falls on the wall.
- Ask the children: 'What do you think this is? How do you know?'
- Now the children take turns in being the shadow maker.

You could also try experimenting with shadow shapes formed by your hands, such as birds, insects, animals and monsters. Making shadow portraits or silhouettes with the children is also a successful activity.

Re-cycle

Early Learning Goals for:

- personal, social and emotional development (PSED): behaviour and self control

- knowledge and understanding of the world (KUW): designing and making.

This is an opportunity to introduce the children to the importance of recycling as part of taking responsibility and caring for the environment.

This activity creates a working context for bikes, providing opportunities for children to negotiate and agree how and when they are used.

- Help the children to decide where an outside construction area will be created. Discuss access, space for building and storage of building materials. Talk about the different kinds of building materials they might collect and use in this area.
- These could include:
    - cardboard cylinders from carpet shops
    - plastic guttering
    - planks and off cuts of wood
    - bricks and stones
    - wheels and tyres
    - cardboard boxes and plastic crates
    - netting, fabric and plastic sheeting
- Think about where you store these reclaimed construction materials so the children can access them easily. Help the children to draw up some rules for the area so resources are stored in an ordered way.
- Encourage the children to make some signs that show these rules and also include some safety warnings.
- Talk with the children about the different vehicles that might visit the construction area, including a recycling lorry, a delivery truck, a plumber's or electrician's van.
- Help them to design and make accessories to customise

the bikes. Talk about responsible driving, speed limits and respect for pedestrians and building workers.

You could also try devising a Highway Code for the setting. Link this with your work on road safety. Develop the children's understanding of recycling and care for the environment by setting up a compost bin.

Key points

- Citizenship for young children means developing self-awareness and self-confidence, learning how to play and work well with others and recognising his or her place in the wider community.
- Exploration and investigation provide an ideal context for fostering the dispositions and attitudes of a good citizen.
- Citizenship involves responsibilities to oneself, to others and for the natural and built environment.
- An environment for citizenship helps children to be independent and self reliant.

Bibliography

References

Association for Science Education (ASE) (2001) *Be Safe*. ASE, Hatfield.

Brunton P and Thornton L (2006) *Exploring Together – Inspiring Family Learning*. Featherstone Education, Lutterworth

Duffy B (1998) *Supporting Creativity and Imagination in the Early Years*. Open University Press, Buckingham

Farrow S (2001) *The Really Useful Science Book*. Routledge Falmer, London Featherstone Education, Lutterworth

Featherstone S, Bailey R (2002) *Foundations for Independence: Developing independent learning in the Foundation Stage*. Featherstone Education, Lutterworth

Guidici C, Rinaldi C, Krechevsky M (eds) (2001) *Making learning visible. Children as individual and group learners*. Reggio Children, Italy

Thornton L, Brunton P (2005) *Understanding the Reggio Approach*. David Fulton, London

Thornton L, Brunton P (2006) *Bringing the Reggio Approach to your early years setting*. David Fulton, London

Thornton L, Brunton P (2003) *The Little Book of Light and Shadow*. Featherstone Education, Lutterworth

Thornton L, Brunton P (2005) *The Little Book of Seasons*. Featherstone Education, Lutterworth

Thornton L, Brunton P (2004) *The Little Book of Time and Place*. Featherstone Education, Lutterworth

Thornton L, Brunton P (2006) *The Little Book of Treasureboxes*. Featherstone Education, Lutterworth

Thornton L, Brunton P (2005) *The Little Book of Living Things*. Featherstone Education, Lutterworth

Resources

Mirrors, magnifiers, magnets, torches, Young Explorers kits, gardening tools, lenses, Perry's pooters, Exploring Outdoors kits and light boxes are available from Reflections on Learning. Tel: 01732 225850. www.reflectionsonlearning.co.uk.

Little Books at Home series. In Our Bathroom, In our Kitchen, In our Garden, In Our Community. Ideal starting points for home-based activities with young children. Featherstone Education. Tel: 01858 881212. www.featherstone.uk.com

Websites

www.campaignforlearning.org.uk

www.ase.org.uk Association for Science Education (ASE). Tel: 01707 283000.

www.alcassociates.co.uk Exploring Together. Family workshops exploring the science and technology behind everyday things by Linda Thornton and Pat Brunton. Alc Associates Ltd. Tel: 01872 273492.